PIRANHAS KEEPER'S HANDBOOK: A day by day guide to caring for your piranhas.

Rowan M. Hart

Published by AquaKind Press, 2025.

While every precaution has been taken in the preparation of this book, the publisher assumes no responsibility for errors or omissions, or for damages resulting from the use of the information contained herein.

PIRANHAS KEEPER'S HANDBOOK: A DAY BY DAY GUIDE TO CARING FOR YOUR PIRANHAS.

First edition. March 28, 2025.

Copyright © 2025 Rowan M. Hart.

Written by Rowan M. Hart.

Table of Contents

Chapter 1: Introduction to Piranhas as Pets 1

Chapter 2: Creating a Safe and Healthy Habitat 3

Chapter 3: Piranha Nutrition: Feeding for Optimal Health 7

Chapter 4: Piranha Behavioral Training and Socialization 11

Chapter 5: Preventive Care and Regular Health Monitoring 15

Chapter 6: Common Piranha Diseases: Identification and Treatment 19

Chapter 7: Skin and Fin Health: Managing Injuries and Infections 23

Chapter 8: Piranha Digestive Health: Preventing and Treating Disorders 27

Chapter 9: Piranha Respiratory and Gill Health 31

Chapter 10: Dealing with Behavioral Issues and Stress 35

Chapter 11: Reproductive Health and Care for Breeding Piranhas 39

Chapter 12: Bonus Recipes for Piranha Health 43

Chapter 13: 30-Day Piranha Care Plan 47

Chapter 14: FAQs and Additional Resources for Piranha Owners 51

Chapter 1: Introduction to Piranhas as Pets

Understanding the Appeal of Piranhas as Pets

Piranhas are among the most intriguing fish species for aquarists, often captivating the imagination with their reputation for ferocity. Despite their fearsome reputation, many piranhas are calm, social creatures that can make fascinating pets when properly cared for. Their predatory nature and dynamic personalities offer a unique and thrilling experience for fish enthusiasts, making them highly desirable for those seeking an exotic and low-maintenance pet.

Piranhas are particularly popular among experienced aquarists who appreciate the challenge of maintaining their specific care requirements and creating an ideal environment for them. For those with the right resources and commitment, keeping piranhas as pets can offer a rewarding experience. Their social behavior, feeding habits, and distinctive physical features are key aspects that draw people to them. However, understanding their true nature and proper care needs is critical to providing a safe and healthy environment for them.

While they are often portrayed as dangerous, most piranhas are quite docile when given adequate space, a balanced diet, and proper tank mates. This chapter will explore what it takes to care for piranhas, helping you understand their appeal and how to decide if a piranha is the right pet for you.

The Natural History and Behavior of Piranhas

Piranhas belong to the family Characidae, which is a diverse group of fish that includes over 30 species. Native to the rivers and lakes of South America, piranhas have evolved to thrive in the warm, slow-moving waters of the Amazon, Orinoco, and Paraná basins. These environments provide a rich ecosystem full of prey, from insects to smaller fish, which form the bulk of their diet.

Piranhas are characterized by their sharp teeth and powerful jaws, built for scavenging and hunting. Most species of piranha are omnivores, feeding on a diet of plants, fruits, and fish. They are often depicted as aggressive predators, but in reality, their aggression is typically reserved for food competition, territorial disputes, and self-defense.

In the wild, piranhas often live in schools, which helps them stay safe from larger predators. However, in captivity, they may display more territorial behavior, especially in smaller tanks or if they do not have enough space. Understanding their social needs is crucial when keeping piranhas in an aquarium. Though their aggressive nature is overstated, piranhas do require careful attention to their social structure, and it's essential to provide them with an environment that meets their behavioral needs.

Determining if a Piranha is the Right Pet for You

Before deciding whether to keep a piranha as a pet, it's essential to evaluate whether your lifestyle and resources align with the care demands of these fish. Piranhas are best suited for experienced aquarists who are willing to provide a controlled and stable environment.

Considerations to keep in mind:

- **Space and Environment:** Piranhas require large tanks, often 50 gallons or more, depending on the species. A larger tank will help mitigate territorial aggression and provide enough room for the fish to swim freely. It is crucial to create a setup that mimics their natural habitat, with plenty of hiding spots, live plants, and strong filtration systems to maintain water quality.
- **Feeding Requirements:** Piranhas can have specific dietary needs, requiring both protein and plant matter in

their diet. Their diet should consist of high-quality pellets, live or frozen fish, and occasional plant matter. Regular feedings and maintaining a clean tank are vital to their health.
- **Behavioral Considerations:** While piranhas are often seen as aggressive, this is more of a territorial behavior. Understanding how to maintain peaceful relationships between tankmates and controlling their environment is crucial for keeping piranhas with other species.
- **Long-term Commitment:** Piranhas can live up to 10-15 years in captivity, so caring for one requires a long-term commitment. Their health, behavior, and environment need continuous attention and adjustment as they grow.

If you are an experienced aquarist with ample space and time, piranhas can be an exciting addition to your aquarium collection. However, they may not be suitable for novice owners due to their specialized needs and the potential for aggressive behaviors if not managed properly.

Setting Up the Ideal Environment for Your Piranha

Creating an ideal environment for your piranha is essential to ensure it thrives in captivity. Piranhas, like all fish, are sensitive to changes in their environment, so setting up the tank correctly from the start is crucial for their long-term health and happiness.

Tank Size and Setup:

- Piranhas need a tank that is large enough to accommodate their territorial and swimming needs. A minimum of 50 gallons is recommended for a small group, but larger species or schools will require even more space.
- The tank should be equipped with a high-quality filtration system that can handle the bioload produced by these active fish. Piranhas produce a lot of waste, so maintaining water quality is essential to prevent disease.

Water Parameters:

- Piranhas are native to warm, tropical waters, so they require a water temperature between 75°F and 80°F (24°C-27°C). The pH should be kept between 6.5 and 7.5, as they prefer slightly acidic to neutral water.
- Ammonia and nitrate levels should be kept as low as possible, with regular water changes (typically 25-30% per week) to maintain optimal water quality.

Tank Decor:

- Piranhas feel more secure in tanks with plenty of hiding places, such as rocks, driftwood, and plants. Live plants can also help with water quality but should be hardy, as piranhas may uproot them.
- Substrate can be sandy or fine gravel, but it's essential to avoid sharp materials that could injure the fish's sensitive bodies.

Tankmates:

- Piranhas are best kept with other piranhas, as they may become territorial and aggressive toward different species. However, with careful monitoring, they can be kept with other large, robust species that can hold their own in terms of size and temperament.

By following these guidelines and maintaining a stable, clean, and well-maintained aquarium, you can create an ideal environment where your piranhas will feel safe and comfortable, allowing them to thrive in their new home.

Chapter 2: Creating a Safe and Healthy Habitat

Designing an Aquarium Suited to Piranhas

Creating the perfect habitat for your piranhas is one of the most critical steps in ensuring their health and well-being. Piranhas, being territorial and often aggressive, require a spacious and well-planned aquarium that mimics their natural environment in the wild. A poorly designed habitat can lead to stress, aggression, or illness, all of which can affect the health of your fish.

Tank Size and Shape:

- **Tank Size:** Piranhas require a large tank to accommodate their active nature and territorial behavior. A minimum of 50 gallons is recommended for a single piranha or a small group. As they grow, a tank size of 75 to 100 gallons is ideal to provide enough space for swimming and reduce territorial aggression. Larger species of piranhas will require even more space.
- **Tank Shape:** A long tank is preferable to a tall tank, as piranhas are horizontal swimmers. A longer tank will allow them to move freely and establish territories within the aquarium. A length of 4 feet or more is ideal for a group of piranhas, providing ample space for them to establish their space and reduce aggression.

Aquarium Setup:

- **Water Flow:** Piranhas prefer calm waters, so while strong filtration is necessary, the flow of water should not be too turbulent. Choose a filtration system that is capable of maintaining water quality while ensuring the current is gentle. A high-quality external filter or canister filter is often the best choice to maintain excellent water clarity.
- **Tank Lid:** Piranhas can sometimes be quite jumpy, especially when startled, so it is important to use a secure lid to prevent them from escaping. This is particularly important if you have a larger tank with a substantial water surface area.

Water Quality, Filtration, and Temperature Control

Maintaining optimal water quality is one of the most crucial aspects of keeping healthy piranhas. These fish are sensitive to changes in their environment, and poor water quality can lead to stress, disease, and shortened lifespans.

Water Quality:

- **pH Levels:** Piranhas thrive in water that is slightly acidic to neutral. A pH level between 6.5 and 7.5 is ideal for most species. Regular testing of water pH is recommended to ensure it stays within the optimal range. Sudden changes in pH can stress piranhas, so it's important to make gradual adjustments if necessary.
- **Ammonia and Nitrites:** Ammonia and nitrites are toxic to fish, and elevated levels can cause serious health issues. It is crucial to monitor the nitrogen cycle in your tank, ensuring that ammonia and nitrites are kept at undetectable levels. Regular water testing is necessary to track these levels, especially in a newly set-up tank.
- **Nitrates:** While nitrates are less toxic than ammonia and nitrites, high levels can still lead to stress and poor

health. Keeping nitrate levels below 20-40 ppm is recommended for piranhas. Regular water changes will help keep nitrate levels in check.

Filtration:

- A high-quality filtration system is essential for maintaining water clarity and removing excess waste from the tank. For piranhas, a canister filter or an external filter is often the best choice, as these systems provide strong, consistent filtration while maintaining a low-current environment.
- **Filtration Capacity:** Aim for a filter that can handle at least 3–5 times the tank's water volume per hour. This ensures that the filter can adequately process waste and maintain a healthy environment.
- **Water Changes:** Even with a good filtration system, regular water changes are necessary to keep the water quality in check. Aim to change 20-30% of the water each week. Make sure to use a water conditioner to remove chlorine and chloramine from tap water.

Temperature Control:

- Piranhas are tropical fish that require warm water to thrive. The ideal water temperature for piranhas is between 75°F and 80°F (24°C-27°C). It is essential to maintain a stable temperature, as sudden fluctuations can cause stress and weaken the fish's immune system.
- A reliable aquarium heater is necessary to maintain consistent water temperatures. Choose a high-quality, fully submersible heater that is properly sized for your tank. Ensure the heater is equipped with a thermostat to regulate the temperature and prevent overheating.

Substrate, Plants, and Decorations for Piranhas

Piranhas are relatively hardy when it comes to tank decor, but the right substrate, plants, and decorations can enhance their habitat and make them feel secure. The goal is to recreate the riverbank environments they naturally inhabit, where they find shelter and protection from larger predators.

Substrate:

- **Material:** Piranhas prefer a fine or medium-gravel substrate that is gentle on their sensitive undersides. Avoid sharp-edged gravel or substrates that could injure your fish. A fine sand or smooth gravel substrate is ideal.
- **Depth:** A substrate depth of 2-3 inches is sufficient to allow for natural behavior, such as scavenging and digging. However, piranhas are unlikely to dig extensively, so it's not necessary to have a deep substrate.

Plants:

- Piranhas are known to uproot plants, so any plants in the aquarium should be sturdy and well-anchored. While piranhas are not known for being particularly plant-eating, providing a few hardy live plants can help improve water quality and offer some hiding places. Plants like Anubias, Java Fern, and Amazon Sword are good choices, as they are robust and can tolerate the conditions found in a piranha tank.
- **Artificial Plants:** If live plants are frequently uprooted, you can use high-quality artificial plants that are safe for aquarium use. These plants can still provide hiding places and decorations without the risk of being destroyed.

Decorations:

- Piranhas enjoy having hiding places where they can retreat when they feel threatened. Driftwood, rocks, and caves can provide excellent hiding spots and create territories within the tank.
- **Natural Look:** To create an authentic environment, try to replicate the piranha's natural habitat with pieces of driftwood, rocks, and leaf litter. The decor should provide enough cover for each fish to establish a personal space.

Lighting:

- Piranhas prefer dim lighting, as bright lights can stress them out. Use low-wattage aquarium lights or LED strips that simulate a natural, overcast environment. Lighting should also be on a timer to ensure that piranhas have a consistent day/night cycle.

Common Tank Mates and Avoiding Territorial Conflicts

While piranhas are often viewed as solitary and aggressive creatures, they can live peacefully with certain tank mates under the right conditions. However, choosing the wrong tank mates can result in aggression, stress, or even predation.

Suitable Tank Mates:

- **Other Piranhas:** The best tank mates for piranhas are other piranhas. A school of piranhas can help distribute aggression and allow the fish to feel more secure in their environment. However, only keep piranhas of similar size together to prevent bullying.
- **Large, Peaceful Fish:** Larger, peaceful fish that can hold their own in a tank may also be suitable companions. Species like large catfish (e.g., Plecostomus or Redtail Catfish) or peaceful cichlids may work well, but only if the tank is large enough to accommodate them.

Avoiding Territorial Conflicts:

- **Tank Size:** The larger the tank, the less likely you are to encounter territorial conflicts. A larger tank allows piranhas to establish their space without constantly competing for territory.
- **Tank Setup:** Provide plenty of hiding spaces and visual barriers to reduce aggression. The more territory each piranha can claim, the less likely they are to fight.
- **Avoiding Small or Delicate Fish:** Avoid keeping small fish or those that may be perceived as prey. Species like tetras, guppies, or goldfish are not suitable tank mates for piranhas, as they may be attacked and eaten.

By carefully selecting tank mates, providing ample space, and designing the tank with the appropriate decorations and hiding places, you can help minimize territorial conflicts and ensure that your piranhas live in a harmonious environment.

Chapter 3: Piranha Nutrition: Feeding for Optimal Health

Understanding the Dietary Needs of Piranhas

Proper nutrition is essential for the health and vitality of your piranhas. These predatory fish are naturally carnivorous, and their diet in captivity should reflect the nutrient composition they would encounter in the wild. A well-balanced diet helps maintain a piranha's immune system, promotes growth, and enhances its natural behavior.

Natural Diet in the Wild: In their natural habitat, piranhas are opportunistic feeders, hunting in packs to catch small fish, insects, and occasionally, fruit or plants. They are adapted to a high-protein diet, and their sharp teeth are designed for ripping and tearing through their prey. This carnivorous nature should be reflected in their diet when kept in an aquarium, but some adjustments are necessary for their captive care.

Nutritional Requirements:

- **Protein:** Piranhas require a high-protein diet to maintain muscle mass and support their active lifestyle. Protein should make up a large percentage of their diet—at least 40-50%.
- **Fat:** Piranhas also need healthy fats to sustain energy levels. Fish oils, krill, and other marine-based fats are excellent sources.
- **Vitamins and Minerals:** While protein and fat are essential, vitamins and minerals, particularly calcium and vitamin D, are necessary for proper bone health and immune function.
- **Carbohydrates:** Unlike herbivores, piranhas require minimal carbohydrates. Their diet should primarily consist of protein, with small amounts of carbohydrates from whole food sources like vegetables or insects, rather than grains.

Types of Food: Natural Versus Commercial Options

Providing a varied and balanced diet is crucial to ensure your piranhas receive all the nutrients they need. There are two primary sources of food: natural (live or frozen) and commercial options (pellets and freeze-dried food). Both have their advantages, and a combination of the two is often the best approach.

Natural Food:

- **Live Food:** Offering live food can stimulate a piranha's hunting instincts, promoting natural behaviors like chasing and capturing prey. Common live foods include feeder fish (such as minnows or goldfish), live insects, and worms. However, it's crucial to ensure that live food is free of parasites or diseases that could harm your piranhas. Always purchase live food from a reputable source to avoid contamination.
- **Frozen Food:** Frozen food is a more convenient option that still offers the nutritional value of live food. Common frozen options include shrimp, krill, worms, and small fish. These foods can be thawed and fed to your piranhas in appropriate portions. Freezing preserves the nutritional value and eliminates the risks associated with live food.

Commercial Food:

- **Pellets and Flakes:** High-quality pellets are formulated to meet the dietary needs of carnivorous fish like piranhas. These foods are typically rich in protein, vitamins, and minerals. When selecting pellets, look for ones designed specifically for carnivorous fish, as general fish food may not provide the necessary nutrients. It's important to choose brands that list high-quality animal protein as the first ingredient, rather than fillers like grains.
- **Freeze-Dried Foods:** Freeze-dried options, such as bloodworms, brine shrimp, and krill, are convenient and nutrient-dense. They offer the same nutritional benefits as frozen foods but have a longer shelf life. However, freeze-dried foods can cause bloating if fed in excess, so it's important to regulate portion sizes.

Combining Natural and Commercial Food:

- A balanced diet often involves combining both natural and commercial foods. A base of high-quality pellets or freeze-dried food can be supplemented with occasional live or frozen food to provide variety and enrichment. Offering a mix of both ensures that your piranhas get a variety of nutrients and keeps mealtime engaging.

Feeding Schedules and Portion Control

Feeding your piranhas on a consistent schedule is vital for their health. Overfeeding or underfeeding can both lead to significant health issues, including obesity, malnutrition, or water quality problems from uneaten food. Developing a feeding routine will not only help regulate your fish's health but also maintain water quality in the aquarium.

Feeding Frequency:

- **Young Piranhas:** Juvenile piranhas need to be fed more frequently than adults. They should be fed once or twice a day. A smaller portion that they can consume in 5-10 minutes is ideal. This helps to support their growth and development.
- **Adult Piranhas:** Adult piranhas generally require fewer feedings. Once a day or even every other day is sufficient. Adult piranhas are less active than juveniles and do not require as many calories. Their feeding schedule should consist of larger portions, but it's essential not to overfeed.

Portion Control:

- **Portion Size:** The general rule of thumb for portion control is to offer as much food as your piranha can eat in 5-10 minutes. Remove any uneaten food after this time to prevent water contamination.
- **Avoid Overfeeding:** Overfeeding can lead to obesity, which is a common problem in captive piranhas. It can also result in excess waste, which negatively impacts water quality. Only offer food that can be consumed in a reasonable amount of time and adjust portions based on your piranha's size and activity level.
- **Monitor Weight and Health:** Regularly assess your piranha's body condition. A healthy piranha should have a well-defined, streamlined body shape. If your fish is looking overly round or lethargic, it could be a sign of overfeeding or a dietary imbalance.

Holistic Dietary Supplements and Treats

In addition to a regular diet, you can provide your piranhas with holistic supplements and treats to promote overall health. These additions are not substitutes for a balanced diet but can support immune function, growth, and vitality.

Natural Supplements:

- **Garlic:** Garlic is a natural immune booster and can be added to food to help strengthen your piranha's immune system. It can be finely chopped or mashed and mixed with frozen or live food. Some commercial foods may also include garlic as an ingredient for its health benefits.
- **Spirulina:** This nutrient-rich algae is full of antioxidants, vitamins, and minerals. While it is more commonly associated with herbivores, some carnivorous fish like piranhas can benefit from small amounts of spirulina. It can be mixed with other foods to provide additional nutritional support.
- **Krill and Fish Oil:** Omega-3 fatty acids found in krill and fish oils can help improve the health of a piranha's skin and scales, as well as support overall cardiovascular health. You can offer krill or fish oil as a supplement to your fish's diet, or find foods that contain these nutrients.

Treats:

- **Live Insects:** Live food, such as mealworms, crickets, and earthworms, can serve as occasional treats for your piranha. These insects mimic the natural hunting experience and provide additional nutritional benefits.
- **Frozen or Freeze-Dried Shrimp:** Frozen or freeze-dried shrimp make excellent treats, providing a protein boost and promoting natural predatory behavior.

Enrichment: Offering a variety of foods not only helps provide a balanced diet but also stimulates your piranha's natural hunting instincts. Occasionally changing up the food source can prevent boredom and promote a healthy appetite.

When to Seek Veterinary Advice Regarding Nutrition

While piranhas are relatively easy to feed, there are times when you should seek veterinary advice regarding their diet.

Signs of Nutritional Imbalance:

- **Weight Loss or Lack of Growth:** If your piranha is not gaining weight or seems to be losing weight despite adequate feeding, it could indicate a nutritional deficiency or an underlying health problem.
- **Obesity:** If your piranha appears overweight and lethargic, it could be a sign of overfeeding or an inappropriate diet. An aquarium veterinarian can help you adjust your feeding routine and suggest dietary changes.
- **Digestive Issues:** If your piranha is experiencing bloating, constipation, or difficulty swimming, it could be a sign of improper digestion. These symptoms might arise from overfeeding, feeding inappropriate food, or food that is too large or difficult to digest.

Parasites or Disease: If you notice changes in your piranha's behavior, such as a loss of appetite, lethargy, or abnormal swimming, it could be a sign of illness related to diet. Seeking a veterinarian's advice can help you address potential parasitic infections, digestive issues, or other health concerns.

By providing a varied and well-balanced diet, and paying attention to your piranha's nutritional needs, you can ensure that your fish remains healthy and active. Regular feeding, portion control, and occasional supplementation can support their immune system, growth, and overall well-being. However, if you notice any signs of illness or dietary problems, consulting with an aquarium vet is always a good idea to prevent further complications.

Chapter 4: Piranha Behavioral Training and Socialization

Understanding Piranha Behavior and Communication

Piranhas are fascinating creatures, known for their sharp teeth and predatory instincts, but they are also highly social and intelligent. Understanding their natural behaviors and how they communicate with each other and their environment is key to fostering a healthy relationship with your pet piranhas.

Natural Behavior: Piranhas in the wild typically live in groups, or schools, where they can collectively hunt and protect each other from predators. While they are often portrayed as aggressive, their behavior is more nuanced, with aggression usually being a response to threats or competition for resources. Piranhas are also opportunistic feeders, and their interactions with each other often revolve around food and territory.

Communication: Piranhas communicate primarily through body language, including postures, movements, and occasional vocalizations (such as grunts or clicks). Their fins and body position convey a great deal of information about their mood. For example:

- **Flared Fins:** This can indicate territorial behavior or aggression.
- **Head or Body Tilting:** This may be a sign of curiosity or stress.
- **Chasing or Biting:** If piranhas chase each other or nip at one another, it can be a sign of competition or aggression over territory or food.

Recognizing these signals will help you understand when your piranha is stressed, when it's feeling playful, or when it's simply acting out of hunger.

Techniques for Handling Aggression and Territoriality

Piranhas can be territorial and may show aggression, especially in confined spaces or when food is scarce. As an owner, it's important to understand and address aggression, both between piranhas and towards other fish or people.

Identifying Aggression:

- **Fin Displays:** When piranhas feel threatened or territorial, they may display their fins in a flared, defensive manner.
- **Chasing or Nipping:** Aggressive piranhas often chase or nip at one another, which can lead to injury if not managed.
- **Increased Activity:** Aggressive piranhas may become more active or erratic, especially in the presence of food or other environmental stressors.

Dealing with Aggression:

- **Aquarium Size:** Providing ample space is one of the most effective ways to minimize territorial disputes. A larger aquarium allows each piranha to establish its own territory, reducing the likelihood of constant aggression. For multiple piranhas, a minimum of 75-100 gallons per fish is recommended to give them the space they need.

- **Aquarium Design:** Strategic placement of decorations, plants, and hiding spots can also help reduce aggression by giving piranhas places to retreat and establish their own territories.
- **Feeding Routine:** Establishing a consistent feeding schedule can help reduce food-related aggression. Avoid overfeeding, as it can lead to competitive behavior, and always ensure that all piranhas are able to access food at the same time.
- **Individual Attention:** If aggression is frequent, separating particularly aggressive individuals into separate tanks may be necessary.

Addressing Aggression Towards Humans: Piranhas can sometimes exhibit aggression towards humans, especially when they feel threatened. This is often a defense mechanism, so it is important to avoid sudden movements or behavior that might provoke them.

- **Slow Movements:** Approach the aquarium slowly and calmly to avoid startling your piranhas.
- **Avoiding Hands in the Tank:** Piranhas may bite if their space is invaded, so avoid placing your hands in the tank unless absolutely necessary. When cleaning or performing maintenance, use tools designed for aquarium care to avoid putting your hands in the water.

Socializing Piranhas with Other Fish

Piranhas are known to be somewhat aggressive, especially towards smaller fish that resemble prey. However, they can coexist with other species if introduced properly and if the environment is right.

Selecting Compatible Tank Mates: While piranhas are often best kept alone or in species-specific groups, certain fish can make suitable tank mates under the right conditions:

- **Larger Fish:** Larger species that are more aggressive or similar in size to the piranha are often suitable companions. Species like catfish, large tetras, or other large characins may work well in the same tank.
- **Avoid Smaller Fish:** Smaller or slower-moving fish should be avoided as they could be seen as prey. Fish that are too small or fragile may become targets for your piranha, leading to injury or death.
- **Calm Species:** Peaceful fish that do not compete for food or territory may be acceptable companions, but be mindful of the piranha's behavior around them.

Introducing New Tank Mates: Introducing new fish into a piranha tank requires careful planning:

- **Quarantine New Fish:** Before introducing new fish, it is wise to quarantine them for a week or two to ensure they are free from diseases or parasites.
- **Gradual Introduction:** When adding new fish, introduce them slowly to prevent territorial aggression. You can temporarily place the new fish in a separate section of the aquarium or in a floating breeder box to allow the piranhas to adjust to the presence of new tank mates before full integration.
- **Monitor Closely:** Watch the interactions between the piranhas and new fish closely for the first few days. Look for signs of stress or aggression, such as chasing, biting, or excessive hiding, and be ready to separate any overly aggressive piranhas if needed.

Training for Stress Reduction and Comfort

Piranhas are intelligent fish and can be trained to some degree, though their training is different from that of mammals. Training can help reduce stress and encourage healthy behaviors, making it an essential part of your piranha's care routine.

Reducing Stress: Piranhas, like all fish, are sensitive to changes in their environment. Sudden changes in water parameters, temperature, or lighting can cause stress and lead to health issues. By creating a stable environment, you can help reduce the stress levels of your piranha.

- **Stable Environment:** Maintain consistent water parameters, temperature, and lighting to ensure your piranhas feel safe and comfortable.
- **Hideouts and Plants:** Provide plenty of hiding spots and plants in the tank to allow your piranhas to retreat when feeling stressed. These elements can help your fish feel more secure, especially during periods of stress, like water changes or new fish introductions.
- **Minimize Handling:** Avoid unnecessary handling of your piranhas, as frequent disturbances can stress them out. When you do need to interact with them, keep it brief and gentle.

Training Techniques: While piranhas are not typically trained in the same way that mammals or birds are, they can learn to associate certain cues with food or other actions, which can reduce stress during feeding time or tank maintenance.

- **Feeding Training:** Use a feeding routine to train your piranhas to associate specific times of day or actions (like tapping on the glass) with feeding. This can help reduce stress and anxiety during feeding time.
- **Positive Reinforcement:** Just like with other animals, positive reinforcement can be effective in training piranhas. When your piranha behaves in a calm and non-aggressive manner, reward it with a small treat, such as a piece of frozen shrimp or a live worm. Over time, your piranha will begin to associate calm behavior with positive outcomes.

Piranhas, despite their fierce reputation, are fascinating and complex creatures. Understanding their behavior and communication, using effective strategies to handle aggression, and providing opportunities for socialization and training are all key to ensuring your piranhas thrive in captivity. With careful attention to their behavioral needs and a thoughtful approach to their environment and interactions with other fish, you can create a peaceful and harmonious aquarium that fosters both the physical and emotional well-being of your piranhas.

Chapter 5: Preventive Care and Regular Health Monitoring

Recognizing Early Signs of Illness

One of the most important aspects of keeping piranhas healthy is recognizing the early signs of illness. Since piranhas can sometimes hide their symptoms until a condition becomes severe, staying vigilant and proactive can help prevent minor issues from escalating into serious health concerns. Early detection leads to more effective treatment and can significantly improve your piranha's quality of life.

Common Early Signs of Illness in Piranhas:

- **Changes in Appetite:** A loss of appetite or refusal to eat is often one of the first signs that something is wrong. Piranhas are opportunistic feeders, so if they suddenly show no interest in food, it could indicate stress, illness, or a change in water quality.
- **Unusual Swimming Behavior:** Piranhas typically swim in a steady, controlled manner. If you notice erratic swimming, such as swimming in circles, darting around the tank, or difficulty maintaining buoyancy, it could indicate an issue with their health, including problems with the swim bladder or stress.
- **Changes in Appearance:** Pay attention to any changes in your piranha's appearance, such as:
  - **Fading or Darkening Color:** Piranhas can change color slightly depending on their mood, but significant changes may indicate stress or illness.
  - **Physical Damage:** Look for signs of injuries, including torn fins or scars. Piranhas often fight among themselves, and wounds can quickly become infected if not treated.
  - **Bloating or Swelling:** Swelling in the belly, especially in the absence of feeding, may indicate internal issues like parasites, organ failure, or constipation.
  - **Abnormal Skin or Fins:** White spots, redness, or fraying fins are often signs of external parasites, infections, or poor water quality.

Other Warning Signs:

- **Rapid Gasping at the Surface:** This could indicate oxygen deprivation, water quality issues, or gill infections.
- **Unusual Behavior or Aggression:** If your piranha becomes suddenly more aggressive than usual or shows signs of anxiety or distress, it may be due to environmental stressors or an underlying health problem.
- **Labored Breathing:** Any signs of difficulty breathing, such as fast or irregular gill movement, should be taken seriously and may indicate gill infections or water quality issues.

Routine Health Checks: Monitoring Water Quality, Behavior, and Appearance

Routine health checks are essential to keeping your piranhas in optimal health. Regular monitoring of water quality, behavior, and physical appearance ensures that issues are caught early, reducing the risk of illness and stress.

1. Monitoring Water Quality: Maintaining high water quality is one of the most important factors in preventing illness. Piranhas are sensitive to changes in their environment, and poor water quality can lead to a variety of health issues, including skin infections, stress, and respiratory problems. Regularly check and maintain the following water parameters:

- **Ammonia and Nitrite Levels:** Both ammonia and nitrite are toxic to fish, especially in high concentrations. They should always read as zero in a properly cycled tank. Perform regular water tests to monitor these levels.
- **Nitrate Levels:** Nitrates are less toxic but still harmful at high concentrations. Ideally, nitrate levels should stay below 40-50 ppm. Regular water changes help keep these levels in check.
- **pH Levels:** Piranhas prefer slightly acidic to neutral water (pH 6.5-7.5). Test pH levels regularly to ensure consistency.
- **Hardness and Alkalinity:** Maintaining the right water hardness and alkalinity can prevent stress. Piranhas thrive in soft to moderately hard water.
- **Temperature:** Piranhas thrive in water temperatures between 74°F and 80°F (23°C to 27°C). Any major fluctuation can cause stress or weaken their immune systems.

Water Change Schedule: Perform regular water changes (about 25-30% every 2-3 weeks) to help maintain stable water quality and prevent the buildup of harmful substances. During water changes, be sure to clean the substrate, filter, and decorations to remove any debris that could affect water quality.

2. Behavioral Monitoring: Closely monitor your piranhas for any changes in behavior. They may exhibit subtle signs of distress, such as a decrease in activity or abnormal social interactions, before showing more obvious physical signs of illness.

- **Daily Observation:** Spend time observing your piranhas each day to note any differences in behavior. Do they seem lethargic, stressed, or unusually aggressive? Are they eating regularly? These small changes can often signal early health problems.
- **Watch for Aggression:** Increased aggression towards tank mates or excessive isolation from the group can indicate stress, illness, or injury.

3. Physical Appearance Monitoring: Regularly inspect your piranhas for any visible changes. This includes checking for signs of injury, infection, or skin conditions such as redness, sores, or parasites.

- **Fins and Scales:** Look for any fraying of fins or abnormalities in the scales, which may indicate infections or parasites.
- **Belly Area:** Ensure that the belly is not swollen or bloated. Bloating can be a sign of internal parasites, poor digestion, or other internal health problems.

Preventive Treatments and Supplements

Preventive care involves taking proactive measures to ensure your piranhas remain healthy and to reduce the likelihood of disease. This includes maintaining good water quality, providing a balanced diet, and using preventive treatments when necessary.

1. Regular Deworming: Internal parasites are a common issue for fish, including piranhas. Regular deworming is important to keep your fish's digestive system healthy. Natural treatments like garlic can sometimes help with parasitic infections, but if you notice signs of internal parasites, such as bloating, poor appetite, or lethargy, consult with a vet for appropriate medicated treatments.

2. Anti-parasitic Treatments: External parasites such as ich or flukes can affect piranhas, leading to skin lesions, erratic swimming, and breathing difficulties. Using aquarium-safe anti-parasitic treatments can help prevent and treat these issues. Make sure to follow the treatment instructions carefully to avoid harming your fish or destabilizing the water quality.

3. Supplementing Diets with Probiotics: Just like humans, fish can benefit from probiotics. Probiotic supplements can aid in digestion, boost the immune system, and help maintain a healthy gut flora. These supplements are especially helpful if your piranhas have had issues with constipation or digestive problems.

4. Vitamin and Mineral Supplements: Vitamins and minerals play a key role in maintaining the overall health of your piranhas. Supplements can be added to their diet if necessary, particularly if you notice signs of nutritional deficiency, such as poor coloration, lethargy, or weak fins. Vitamin C and D, in particular, can help improve immune function and skin health.

Creating a Care Schedule and Maintaining Good Health Practices

Establishing a regular care schedule is essential to maintaining the long-term health and well-being of your piranhas. By making routine checks and performing regular maintenance, you'll catch potential problems early and provide your fish with a stable environment.

Daily Care Routine:

- **Observe behavior:** Spend at least 15-20 minutes observing your piranhas. Look for any signs of distress or abnormal behavior.
- **Check food intake:** Ensure that all piranhas are eating regularly and that no uneaten food is left in the tank.
- **Ensure water quality:** Quick checks of water temperature and appearance are recommended daily.

Weekly Care Routine:

- **Perform partial water changes (25-30%):** This helps maintain water quality and remove toxins from the tank.
- **Clean the filter:** Clean the aquarium filter to ensure it's functioning properly, but avoid over-cleaning, as this can disrupt beneficial bacteria.
- **Inspect equipment:** Check the tank heater, thermometer, and filter to make sure everything is working correctly.

Monthly Care Routine:

- **Test water quality:** Perform a thorough test of the water for ammonia, nitrites, nitrates, pH, and hardness.
- **Inspect tank and decorations:** Clean any algae buildup on tank walls and decorations, but avoid using harsh chemicals that could harm the piranhas.

Annual Care Routine:

- **Full tank cleaning:** This includes a deep cleaning of all decorations, substrate, and filtration system, and a complete water change.
- **Check for parasites and illnesses:** If you haven't done so in a while, this is a good time to check for parasites and treat them as necessary.

Preventive care and regular health monitoring are essential for ensuring that your piranhas live long, healthy, and stress-free lives. By staying proactive in maintaining water quality, monitoring behavior, and providing preventive treatments, you'll significantly reduce the risk of illness. Additionally, regular observation and creating a well-structured care schedule will help you detect and address any health issues before they become serious. A balanced approach that integrates both natural remedies and medically supported methods will empower you to offer the best possible care for your piranhas.

Chapter 6: Common Piranha Diseases: Identification and Treatment

Common Illnesses and Parasites Affecting Piranhas

Piranhas, like all aquarium fish, are susceptible to a variety of diseases and parasites. While these conditions can often be managed with proper care and attention, it's essential to be familiar with the most common illnesses and parasites that affect piranhas, so you can act quickly if symptoms arise.

1. External Parasites: External parasites are a frequent issue for aquarium fish, including piranhas. These parasites often attach to the skin, gills, or fins and can cause significant discomfort, stress, and illness.

- **Ich (White Spot Disease):** Caused by a protozoan parasite called *Ichthyophthirius multifiliis*, ich is one of the most common and well-known fish diseases. It manifests as small, white cysts or spots on the skin, gills, and fins.
    - **Symptoms:** White, grainy spots on the body or fins, rubbing against objects, increased respiration rate, and lethargy.
    - **Treatment:** Raise the water temperature (to 82-85°F) to speed up the parasite's life cycle, and treat with an anti-ich medication. Salt baths and formalin can also be used in severe cases.
- **Velvet Disease (Oodinium):** This is caused by the protozoan *Oodinium* and results in a golden or rusty coating on the skin. The parasite infects the gills and skin of fish, often leading to suffocation.
    - **Symptoms:** A golden or rusty-colored dust on the skin, labored breathing, loss of appetite, and lethargy.
    - **Treatment:** Velvet disease can be treated by raising the temperature slightly and adding copper-based treatments or formalin. UV sterilizers can also help eradicate the parasites.
- **Flukes (Trematodes):** These parasitic flatworms often target the gills and skin of fish. They are known for causing tissue damage and can lead to more severe infections if untreated.
    - **Symptoms:** Gasping at the surface, inflamed gills, and abnormal swimming behavior.
    - **Treatment:** Use praziquantel or other anti-fluke medications to treat fluke infestations.

2. Internal Parasites: Internal parasites can also infect piranhas, leading to digestive issues, bloating, or weight loss.

- **Roundworms (Nematodes):** These parasites can affect the digestive tract, causing a variety of symptoms like bloating, poor appetite, or even visible worms in the stool.
    - **Symptoms:** Bloating, poor growth, weight loss, and lethargy.
    - **Treatment:** Deworming treatments with anti-nematode medications, such as levamisole or praziquantel, are effective in treating roundworm infestations.
- **Protozoan Infections (e.g., *Hexamita*):** Protozoan infections like *Hexamita* can affect the intestines and cause significant digestive issues in piranhas.
    - **Symptoms:** Diarrhea, weight loss, poor appetite, and sometimes white feces.
    - **Treatment:** Medications like copper sulfate or other anti-protozoan drugs can be used to treat protozoan infections.

3. Bacterial Infections: Bacterial infections can spread quickly in aquarium environments if water quality is not maintained. They can affect both the skin and internal organs of the fish.

- **Fin Rot (Aeromonas spp.):** A bacterial infection that leads to the gradual decay of the fins, tail, and body of the fish. This infection is typically caused by poor water conditions or physical injury.
  - **Symptoms:** Fraying or rotting fins, lesions or ulcers on the body, redness around the infected area.
  - **Treatment:** A combination of antibiotics such as tetracycline, oxytetracycline, or maracyn is effective in treating fin rot. Improving water quality and isolating infected fish can help reduce the spread.
- **Dropsy:** Caused by a bacterial infection, dropsy leads to fluid accumulation inside the body, causing swelling, especially in the abdomen. This condition often indicates serious internal organ damage.
  - **Symptoms:** Swollen belly, pinecone-like appearance of scales, lethargy, and loss of appetite.
  - **Treatment:** Antibiotics like erythromycin or a broad-spectrum antibiotic can help. Dropsy may be a sign of kidney failure or another underlying health issue, so it is important to monitor the condition closely.

4. Fungal Infections: Fungal infections can appear after a fish has suffered an injury, or they can affect weakened fish. The fungus typically grows on the skin or fins and appears as cotton-like growths.

- **Symptoms:** White, cotton-like growths on the skin, fins, or gills. The affected areas may become inflamed or discolored.
  - **Treatment:** Fungal infections can be treated with antifungal medications, such as formalin or copper-based treatments. Keep the water quality high to prevent secondary infections.

Symptoms of Stress, Infection, and Illness

Recognizing the symptoms of stress, infection, or illness early can make a significant difference in your piranha's health. Stress and illness often manifest in similar ways, so it's essential to carefully observe your piranha's behavior and appearance to identify potential issues.

Signs of Stress:

- **Erratic Swimming:** Piranhas may swim erratically or near the water's surface if they are stressed.
- **Excessive Hiding or Isolation:** Stress can cause a piranha to seek refuge in dark areas of the tank or isolate itself from other tank mates.
- **Aggression or Fear:** Piranhas may display more aggression or fear-based behavior when stressed, especially if their environment is too small, overcrowded, or unsuitable.
- **Loss of Appetite:** A stressed fish often refuses to eat, which can weaken its immune system and make it more susceptible to disease.

Signs of Infection:

- **Physical Damage:** Signs such as cuts, sores, or lesions on the body could indicate bacterial infections.
- **Discolored Skin:** Redness, paleness, or the appearance of white spots on the skin are signs that the fish may be suffering from a disease like ich or a bacterial infection.
- **Rapid Breathing or Gasping:** Increased respiration rate or gasping at the surface suggests gill damage, poor water quality, or a gill infection.

Signs of Illness:

- **Lethargy or Lack of Movement:** Piranhas that are ill may become lethargic, spending most of their time near the bottom of the tank or swimming slowly.

- **Swollen Belly or Abnormal Shape:** Bloating or changes in shape may indicate internal infections, like parasites or organ failure.
- **Excessive Mucus Production:** If a piranha is producing excess mucus on its skin, it could be a sign of a bacterial or fungal infection.

Holistic and Medical Approaches to Disease Management

In treating piranha diseases, a balanced approach that combines holistic and medical methods can be highly effective. Holistic treatments focus on enhancing the overall health and immune system of the fish, while medical treatments are used to directly combat specific diseases or infections.

Holistic Approaches:

- **Improved Diet:** A nutritious diet rich in vitamins and minerals strengthens the piranha's immune system, helping it to fight off infections naturally. Offering a varied diet of live, frozen, and high-quality pellet food is essential.
- **Garlic and Herbal Remedies:** Garlic is a natural anti-parasitic and immune-boosting supplement. Adding garlic to the diet (in small amounts) or using garlic-based fish supplements can help prevent and treat minor parasitic infections.
- **Stress Reduction:** Reducing stress through stable water conditions, proper tank setup, and minimal handling can help boost a piranha's immune function, making it less likely to develop disease.

Medical Approaches:

- **Antibiotics:** For bacterial infections, such as fin rot or dropsy, antibiotics are often necessary to treat the illness. These can be administered directly to the water or through medicated food.
- **Anti-parasitic Treatments:** If your piranha is infected with parasites (external or internal), specialized anti-parasitic medications, such as praziquantel, copper sulfate, or formalin, can help eliminate the parasites from the fish and tank.
- **Salt Treatments:** Aquarium salt can be used to treat minor wounds, stress, or as a preventive for external parasites. Salt works by promoting osmoregulation and reducing stress on the fish.

When to Consult a Veterinarian for Diagnostics and Treatment

While many common diseases and health issues can be managed at home, there are times when it's best to seek professional help. Veterinary intervention should be considered if:

- **Symptoms Persist:** If your piranha's symptoms do not improve after using over-the-counter treatments or holistic remedies, it may require a more in-depth diagnosis and prescription medication.
- **Severe Symptoms:** If your piranha exhibits severe symptoms such as prolonged lethargy, swelling, or unusual growths, a veterinarian will be able to perform diagnostics like a physical examination, skin scraping, or blood tests to identify the underlying issue.
- **Unresponsive to Treatment:** If you've been treating a condition without success, a veterinarian can help you identify if the right treatment was used or if a different condition is at play.
- **Multiple Fish Affected:** If you have multiple fish displaying similar symptoms, there may be a widespread issue in the tank that requires professional attention.

A qualified fish veterinarian can provide the most accurate diagnosis and treatment plan, ensuring that your piranha receives the best care possible.

Chapter 7: Skin and Fin Health: Managing Injuries and Infections

Treating Cuts, Fin Rot, and Fungal Infections

The skin and fins of piranhas are crucial for their health and mobility, but they are also highly susceptible to injuries and infections. Understanding how to properly treat these conditions will help you keep your piranha healthy and reduce the risk of long-term damage.

1. Cuts and Scratches: Piranhas can sustain cuts or scratches from rough objects in the tank, aggressive interactions with other fish, or while hunting or scavenging. While minor abrasions typically heal on their own, deeper cuts can become infected if left untreated.

- **Treatment:**
  - **Rinse the wound gently**: If you notice a cut or scratch, rinse the affected area with aquarium water to remove any debris or dirt. Avoid using tap water, as it may contain harmful chemicals like chlorine.
  - **Salt Baths**: A salt bath can be helpful for promoting healing and preventing infection. Use aquarium salt and dilute it to the appropriate concentration. Ensure the piranha is only in the salt bath for a brief period (usually no more than 10-15 minutes).
  - **Antibiotic Treatments**: If the wound looks infected, an antibiotic treatment like *Maracyn* or *Kanamycin* can be used to prevent bacteria from taking hold. These treatments are available in liquid form and can be added to the tank water.
- **Prevention:**
  - **Aquarium Setup**: Ensure that the tank has smooth, rounded decorations and objects that won't injure your piranha. Avoid sharp edges, rocks, or plants with rough surfaces.
  - **Tank Mates**: Aggressive behavior from other fish in the tank can lead to physical injury. Monitor interactions, and if necessary, separate aggressive individuals.

2. Fin Rot: Fin rot is a bacterial infection that often appears after a piranha experiences an injury or stress. It can cause the fins to appear ragged, discolored, or even begin to deteriorate.

- **Symptoms:**
  - Fins look frayed, torn, or rotting away.
  - Red or inflamed areas near the edges of the fins.
  - A general decline in the piranha's activity or appetite.
- **Treatment:**
  - **Increase Water Quality**: Begin by ensuring the water quality is optimal. Poor water conditions are a major factor in fin rot, so check ammonia, nitrite, and nitrate levels. Perform water changes as needed.
  - **Antibiotic Treatment**: If the fin rot is due to bacterial infection, use a broad-spectrum antibiotic like *Maracyn* or *Melafix* to treat the tank water or administer through medicated food.
  - **Salt Baths**: Use salt baths to promote healing of the affected fin areas and reduce the likelihood of further infection. A salt concentration of 1 tablespoon per gallon of water is often recommended.
- **Prevention:**
  - **Avoid Overcrowding**: Too many fish in the tank can create stress and increase the risk of injury and infection. Ensure the

tank is appropriately sized for your piranha.
- **Maintain Proper Filtration**: A well-functioning filtration system helps maintain good water quality and reduces the risk of bacterial infections.
- **Monitor for Aggression**: Aggressive behavior from tank mates can cause physical harm and stress, leading to fin rot. Monitor interactions and separate overly aggressive fish.

3. Fungal Infections: Fungal infections are commonly seen after a piranha sustains an injury or is subjected to poor water conditions. These infections typically appear as a white, cotton-like growth on the skin or fins and can quickly lead to severe complications if not treated.

- **Symptoms:**
  - White, cotton-like growth on the skin, fins, or gills.
  - Swollen or inflamed areas around the infection.
  - Lethargy, loss of appetite, and decreased activity.
- **Treatment:**
  - **Antifungal Medications**: Commercial antifungal treatments, such as formalin or copper sulfate, can be used to treat fungal infections. These treatments are available in liquid form and are added directly to the aquarium water.
  - **Salt Baths**: As with other skin conditions, salt baths can help reduce the spread of the fungus and promote healing. Use aquarium salt at the proper dilution rate.
  - **Remove Infected Fish**: If you have multiple fish in the tank, it may be necessary to isolate the infected piranha to prevent the fungus from spreading.
- **Prevention:**
  - **Keep Water Conditions Stable**: Fungus tends to thrive in poor water conditions, so maintaining proper filtration and consistent water parameters is essential for preventing fungal growth.
  - **Limit Stress**: Stress weakens the immune system and makes piranhas more susceptible to infections. Minimize disruptions in the tank, maintain stable water temperatures, and avoid overcrowding.

Preventing Injury in a Tank Environment

A key component of maintaining healthy skin and fins is creating a safe and stress-free environment. Preventing injuries from occurring in the first place is the most effective approach to managing piranha health.

1. Proper Tank Setup:

- **Decorations and Substrate:** Choose smooth decorations and rocks with no sharp edges. Opt for soft, rounded decorations that your piranha can interact with without risk of injury. Avoid using decorations that could easily break and cause injury.
- **Substrate:** Gravel or substrate should be smooth and fine, as rough or sharp substrate can injure the skin or fins of your piranha. Consider using sand or small, rounded pebbles to prevent accidental cuts.

2. Tank Size and Space:

- **Appropriate Tank Size:** Piranhas are territorial and need space to swim freely. Providing a spacious aquarium helps reduce aggression and stress. Ensure the tank is large enough to accommodate the number of fish and allows for adequate swimming space.
- **Territorial Behavior:** Piranhas are known for being aggressive, especially during feeding or breeding. To reduce

the risk of injury, avoid overcrowding the tank and try to limit tank mates that might trigger aggressive behavior.

3. Handling Piranhas with Care:

- **Minimize Stressful Interactions:** Piranhas should only be handled if absolutely necessary. Stressful handling can lead to injuries, stress, and weakened immune responses. If handling is required for tank maintenance or treatment, ensure that the fish is carefully caught and quickly returned to the water.

4. Monitoring Tank Mates:

- **Compatibility:** Not all fish are compatible with piranhas. Avoid keeping other fish that are too small, as they may become prey, leading to stress and potential injury. Conversely, overly aggressive tank mates can also cause harm to your piranha.

Natural Remedies and Commercial Treatments

Both natural and commercial treatments can play a vital role in treating injuries, infections, and skin conditions in piranhas. A holistic approach, combining the strengths of both methods, is often the most effective.

Natural Remedies:

- **Garlic:** Garlic is known for its antibacterial and antifungal properties. Adding garlic to your piranha's diet can help boost its immune system and prevent minor infections.
- **Aloe Vera:** Aloe vera is a natural remedy for minor cuts and scrapes. You can use aloe vera gel to treat small injuries, applying it directly to the affected area to soothe and promote healing.
- **Salt:** Aquarium salt is a gentle, natural treatment for fungal and bacterial infections. It can help reduce inflammation and improve the fish's overall immune response.
- **Herbal Remedies:** Certain herbs like tea tree oil and neem extract have natural antibacterial and antifungal properties. Be sure to dilute them properly before using them in the aquarium.

Commercial Treatments:

- **Antibiotics:** As mentioned earlier, medications such as *Maracyn* and *Kanamycin* are commonly used for treating bacterial infections like fin rot. These medications are available at pet stores and aquarium suppliers.
- **Antifungal Medications:** Products like *CopperSafe* or *Malachite Green* are commonly used to treat fungal infections in aquarium fish.
- **Healing Ointments:** Some specialized ointments, like *Melafix* or *Pimafix*, are specifically designed for treating fish injuries and skin infections. These are applied directly to the water to help speed up the healing process.

Understanding When Medical Intervention Is Required

While minor injuries or infections can often be treated at home with natural remedies or over-the-counter medications, certain situations require professional intervention. It's important to know when to seek help from a veterinarian or fish health specialist:

1. Persistent Symptoms: If the injury or infection doesn't improve within a few days of treatment, or if symptoms worsen, seek veterinary assistance. This could indicate a more severe infection or complication.

2. Severe Injuries: Deep cuts or large wounds that don't heal quickly may require more intensive medical treatment, such as stitches or prescription antibiotics.

3. Rapid Spread of Infection: If multiple fish in the tank are showing signs of infection, or if the infection spreads quickly, consult a veterinarian to ensure proper diagnosis and treatment.

4. Difficulty Breathing or Severe Swelling: If your piranha exhibits labored breathing, significant bloating, or swollen areas that seem to worsen over time, veterinary intervention is necessary.

Maintaining healthy skin and fins is an essential part of piranha care. By taking preventive measures to reduce the risk of injury and infection, and by knowing how to treat minor wounds or infections, you can keep your piranha healthy and thriving. When in doubt, balancing natural remedies with commercial treatments, and seeking veterinary advice when necessary, will ensure the best outcomes for your pet.

Chapter 8: Piranha Digestive Health: Preventing and Treating Disorders

Recognizing Signs of Digestive Upset or Constipation

The digestive health of a piranha is essential for its overall well-being. When a piranha suffers from digestive issues, it can lead to discomfort, nutritional deficiencies, and potentially more severe health complications. Understanding the signs of digestive upset and constipation, as well as how to address these issues, will help you keep your piranha in optimal health.

1. Signs of Digestive Upset: Digestive upset can manifest in several ways. It's important to observe your piranha's behavior, eating habits, and physical appearance to identify potential issues early.

- **Loss of Appetite:** If your piranha suddenly stops eating or refuses food, it could be a sign of digestive distress or illness.
- **Swollen Abdomen:** A bloated or distended belly can indicate a variety of digestive problems, including constipation, bloat, or even internal parasites.
- **Unusual Feces:** The appearance of the feces can reveal a lot about your piranha's digestive health. If the stool is unusually small, hard, or irregular in shape, it may indicate constipation or improper digestion.
- **Lethargy and Reduced Activity:** Digestive discomfort often leads to lethargy or a decrease in normal swimming behavior. If your piranha is unusually still or hides more than usual, digestive distress might be the cause.
- **Floating or Sinking Issues:** Piranhas experiencing severe digestive issues, like bloat, may either float to the surface or sink to the bottom of the tank, due to imbalances in their swim bladder or gas buildup in the intestines.

2. Signs of Constipation: Constipation is one of the most common digestive issues piranhas face. This can occur due to poor diet, lack of fiber, or feeding too much protein-rich food.

- **Hard, Small Feces:** If the piranha's stool is small, hard, and infrequent, this could be a sign of constipation.
- **Abdominal Bloating:** A swollen abdomen or visible signs of bloating often accompany constipation, as undigested food accumulates in the intestines.
- **Reluctance to Eat:** While constipation itself might not always result in a loss of appetite, some piranhas may eat less when feeling discomforted by constipation.

Holistic Remedies for Digestive Health

Before turning to medications, several natural remedies can help promote healthy digestion and alleviate issues like constipation. Holistic care focuses on nourishing the body in a way that supports long-term health and comfort.

1. Fasting: If you notice signs of digestive upset or constipation, consider fasting your piranha for a short period (typically 24–48 hours). This gives the digestive system time to reset and clear any blockages. Fasting can also encourage the piranha to pass any undigested food or waste in its system. However, ensure that the water quality remains pristine during this period, as a dirty tank can worsen digestive issues.

2. Fiber-Rich Foods: A diet that includes fiber can aid digestion and prevent constipation. While piranhas are primarily carnivorous, you can introduce fiber-rich foods in moderation to support their gastrointestinal health.

- **Vegetables**: Soft greens like spinach, zucchini, and peas can be offered in small amounts. You can blanch vegetables (boil briefly and cool) to make them easier for the piranha to eat.
- **Plant Matter in Diet**: While piranhas typically prefer meat, including small amounts of plant matter in their diet may help regulate their digestive processes. Foods like dandelion greens or seaweed can provide necessary fiber.

3. Epsom Salt Baths: Epsom salt baths are a natural remedy that can help relieve constipation in fish by promoting water retention in the intestines. Dissolve a small amount of Epsom salt in aquarium water (around 1 teaspoon per gallon) and place your piranha in this bath for 10–15 minutes. This method helps to gently relieve constipation by easing the passage of waste through the digestive system.

4. Garlic: Garlic is known for its ability to boost the immune system and aid in digestion. Offering small amounts of crushed garlic in your piranha's food may support gut health and help alleviate mild digestive issues.

5. Probiotics: Probiotics are beneficial bacteria that support a healthy gut flora. Adding probiotic supplements to your piranha's food or water can promote digestion and help maintain balance in the digestive tract. You can purchase fish-safe probiotics, or you may choose to make your own probiotic-enriched fish food by fermenting certain ingredients.

6. A Balanced Diet: Ensure that your piranha is receiving a well-rounded diet that includes a mix of protein (meat, fish, or worms) and occasional plant matter. Overfeeding protein-rich foods can lead to digestive blockages or issues like constipation. Balance is key in promoting healthy digestion.

Medical Treatments for Gastrointestinal Issues

While holistic remedies can often be effective, more severe cases of digestive issues may require medical intervention. Common medical treatments for gastrointestinal problems in piranhas include antibiotics, anti-parasitic medications, and other specialized treatments.

1. Antibiotics for Bacterial Infections: In cases where digestive issues are caused by bacterial infections (such as those affecting the gut or liver), your piranha may require antibiotic treatment. **Furan-2** and **Kanamycin** are commonly used to treat bacterial infections that affect the digestive system.

- **How it works:** These antibiotics work by targeting and eliminating harmful bacteria in the piranha's system, allowing the fish to recover from infections that may be impairing digestion.
- **When to use:** Antibiotics are recommended when digestive issues are accompanied by symptoms like swelling, loss of appetite, lethargy, or irregular feces that don't improve with natural remedies.

2. Anti-Parasitic Medications: Parasites, such as intestinal worms, can often cause gastrointestinal issues in piranhas. Medications like **Praziquantel** or **CopperSafe** can be used to treat internal parasites.

- **How it works:** Anti-parasitic treatments target and eliminate parasites in the digestive tract. These medications work by disrupting the parasite's ability to function or reproduce, ultimately expelling them from the piranha's system.
- **When to use:** If your piranha is experiencing symptoms like severe bloating, weight loss, or unusual stool (e.g., stringy or mucous-like), a parasitic infection may be the cause.

3. Commercial Digestive Supplements: There are several commercial products specifically designed to improve digestive health in fish. These supplements may contain enzymes, probiotics, or herbs that promote better digestion and help balance gut health. Products such as **Azoo Fish Food Enzymes** are formulated to aid digestion, especially for fish with sluggish digestive systems.

- **How it works:** These supplements provide essential digestive enzymes and beneficial bacteria that help break down food more efficiently, ensuring proper nutrient absorption and reducing digestive distress.
- **When to use:** Use these products if you notice a chronic issue with digestion that natural remedies haven't resolved, or if your piranha is having difficulty breaking down food.

4. Medicated Foods: For persistent digestive issues, medicated foods may be helpful. These foods are infused with medication that targets digestive problems directly and can be fed to the piranha over a period of days. Products like **Metroplex** (a food medication) can help treat gut infections and improve overall digestion.

- **How it works:** Medicated foods deliver treatment directly to the digestive system, ensuring that the medication reaches the source of the problem more effectively.
- **When to use:** Medicated foods are best for cases where the digestive issue is severe and other treatments have not been successful.

Tips for Preventing Common Digestive Issues

Prevention is key to ensuring that your piranha's digestive system remains healthy throughout its life. By incorporating a few best practices into your pet care routine, you can minimize the risk of digestive problems.

1. Maintain Proper Water Quality: Poor water conditions are often the root cause of many digestive and health issues in aquarium fish. Regular water changes, maintaining proper filtration, and ensuring stable water parameters (pH, ammonia, nitrites, nitrates) will help prevent digestive upset.

2. Avoid Overfeeding: Overfeeding is one of the most common causes of constipation in fish. Feed your piranha only what it can consume in a few minutes, once or twice a day. Always remove any uneaten food to avoid water quality issues.

3. Provide a Balanced Diet: A varied diet helps prevent the accumulation of indigestible material in the stomach. Avoid feeding only protein-heavy foods; include plant matter like leafy greens in moderation to help with digestion.

4. Manage Tank Stress: Stress can lead to digestive issues, as it weakens the immune system and disrupts normal bodily functions. Keep your piranha's environment calm, avoid overcrowding, and ensure that tank mates are compatible to reduce stress.

Piranha digestive health is a crucial aspect of overall well-being, and understanding how to prevent, identify, and treat digestive disorders is essential for any piranha owner. Through holistic remedies such as fasting, dietary adjustments, and natural supplements, as well as medically supported treatments like antibiotics and anti-parasitic medications, you can ensure your piranha remains healthy and happy. By maintaining a balanced diet, avoiding overfeeding, and closely monitoring water conditions, you can prevent most digestive issues and keep your piranha in optimal health.

Chapter 9: Piranha Respiratory and Gill Health

Identifying Respiratory Issues in Piranhas
The respiratory health of a piranha is essential to its overall well-being, as it impacts its ability to obtain oxygen and expel carbon dioxide. Respiratory problems in piranhas are often linked to environmental factors, water quality, or infections. Recognizing the early signs of respiratory distress can help you address the issue before it escalates into a more serious condition.

1. Signs of Respiratory Issues:

- **Rapid Gill Movement:** If your piranha is breathing faster than usual, with noticeable rapid gill movement, it may be struggling to obtain sufficient oxygen.
- **Labored Breathing:** Labored or irregular breathing, where the piranha seems to be gasping or struggling for air, is a clear sign of respiratory distress.
- **Mouth Breathing:** A piranha that is primarily breathing through its mouth (as opposed to its gills) may indicate poor water quality or gill issues, such as infection or clogging.
- **Faded or Abnormal Gill Color:** Healthy piranha gills should be a vibrant pink or red. Pale or discolored gills can signal poor oxygenation, illness, or a bacterial infection.
- **Erratic Swimming or Lethargy:** Respiratory distress may cause the fish to swim erratically, float at the water's surface, or rest at the bottom of the tank. This is often accompanied by signs of lethargy or a reluctance to engage in normal activities.

2. Possible Causes of Respiratory Issues:

- **Poor Water Quality:** High levels of ammonia, nitrites, or nitrates, as well as low oxygen levels, can lead to respiratory problems in piranhas.
- **Gill Infections:** Bacterial, fungal, or parasitic infections affecting the gills can impede oxygen absorption.
- **Obstructed Gills:** A build-up of debris, such as uneaten food or waste particles, can block the gills and affect breathing.
- **Stress and Poor Environment:** Overcrowded tanks, incompatible tank mates, or sudden temperature fluctuations can contribute to respiratory distress in piranhas.

Preventive Care for Gills and Breathing Health
Prevention is always better than treatment, and ensuring your piranha's respiratory health starts with proper aquarium management. Maintaining good water quality and an optimal environment will significantly reduce the likelihood of respiratory problems.

1. Maintaining Optimal Water Quality:

- **Regular Water Changes:** Regularly changing the water in your piranha's tank is essential for maintaining clean and oxygen-rich conditions. Aim for a 20-30% water change every week to reduce the buildup of harmful chemicals.

- **Water Filtration:** Invest in a high-quality filter that is capable of removing waste and harmful toxins from the water. Proper filtration is crucial for maintaining good water quality and ensuring healthy gills.
- **Oxygenation:** Make sure that the water is well-oxygenated by using air stones or a good filtration system that promotes surface agitation. Piranhas require oxygen-rich water for optimal respiratory function.
- **Monitor Water Parameters:** Regularly test the water for ammonia, nitrites, nitrates, pH, and temperature. Keeping the water within ideal parameters helps prevent stress and supports healthy gill function.

2. Tank Maintenance and Environment:

- **Avoid Overcrowding:** Overcrowding can lead to poor water quality and increased stress, both of which can negatively impact gill health. Ensure your tank has enough space for each piranha to swim freely.
- **Proper Tank Size:** Piranhas need large tanks to thrive, as their size and territorial behavior require ample space. A 75-gallon tank is a good starting point for one piranha, with additional space needed for each new one.
- **Stable Water Temperature:** Keep the water temperature in the ideal range for piranhas (75-80°F or 24-27°C). Sudden temperature fluctuations can stress the fish, making them more vulnerable to respiratory issues.

3. Regular Health Monitoring:

- **Observe Breathing Patterns:** Regularly observe your piranha for signs of respiratory distress, such as rapid gill movement or labored breathing. Early detection allows for timely intervention.
- **Monitor Behavior:** Behavioral changes, such as lethargy or erratic swimming, should be investigated as potential signs of respiratory problems or other health issues.

Natural Solutions for Gill Problems

When it comes to holistic remedies for respiratory and gill health, natural solutions can often provide relief, particularly for mild or early-stage issues. However, natural remedies should be used in conjunction with regular water maintenance and health monitoring.

1. Salt Baths: A mild salt bath can help alleviate certain gill-related issues by drawing out toxins and promoting the healing of minor infections. You can prepare a salt bath by dissolving aquarium salt in a separate container of water and then placing your piranha in it for 10-15 minutes.

- **How it works:** Salt helps to cleanse the skin and gills of toxins and can assist in reducing inflammation caused by infection or poor water quality.
- **When to use:** Use a salt bath when you observe mild gill irritation or when the piranha seems stressed due to poor water quality. Do not overuse this remedy, as excessive salt exposure can harm the piranha.

2. **Herbal Remedies:** Herbal remedies can be effective for boosting the immune system and promoting respiratory health. You can use herbs like **echinacea** or **garlic** to enhance gill health and reduce the risk of infection.

- **Garlic:** Garlic is known for its natural anti-bacterial properties and can be used to treat minor gill infections. You can crush a small amount of garlic and mix it with your piranha's food or soak it in the tank water.
- **Echinacea:** Echinacea has immune-boosting properties that can help the piranha recover from minor gill infections. You can prepare a diluted herbal solution to add to the tank, ensuring it is fish-safe.

3. Water Conditioner Additives: Some natural water additives can help support gill health by improving water quality and promoting healthy slime coating on the piranha's skin and gills. Look for **Aloe Vera-based water conditioners** that can soothe and protect the gills from irritation or minor damage.

- **How it works:** Aloe vera helps to maintain the piranha's protective slime coat and prevents irritation from poor water conditions or minor injuries.
- **When to use:** Use when you notice the gills becoming irritated, or when water conditions are less than optimal. Regular use can also serve as a preventative measure.

Medical Treatments and When to Consult a Vet

In some cases, respiratory and gill issues may require more intensive medical intervention, particularly if infections or parasites are involved. Recognizing when to seek veterinary advice is key to ensuring your piranha's recovery.

1. Medications for Gill Infections:

- **Antibiotics:** If a bacterial infection is suspected (signs include inflamed or discolored gills, labored breathing, or swelling), a course of antibiotics may be necessary. Medications like **Furan-2** or **Kanamycin** can help treat gill infections caused by bacteria.
- **How it works:** Antibiotics work by targeting and eliminating harmful bacteria in the gills, which can help restore proper respiratory function.
- **When to use:** If you notice significant gill swelling, bleeding, or loss of color, or if the piranha exhibits signs of systemic illness, consult a veterinarian for an accurate diagnosis and appropriate antibiotic treatment.

2. Antifungal Treatments: Fungal infections, such as those caused by **Saprolegnia**, can also affect the gills and lead to respiratory problems. Antifungal treatments, such as **CopperSafe**, can help eliminate these infections.

- **How it works:** Copper-based treatments help to eliminate fungal growth in the gills, reducing inflammation and improving the piranha's ability to breathe.
- **When to use:** If you see fluffy, cotton-like growths on the gills or body, it's time to consult a vet for a proper antifungal treatment.

3. Parasitic Infections: Gill flukes or other parasitic infestations can cause serious respiratory distress in piranhas. Medications like **Praziquantel** are effective for treating parasitic infections.

- **How it works:** These medications target and kill the parasites that infest the gills, allowing for recovery and restoring normal breathing.
- **When to use:** If your piranha is showing signs of excessive mucus production, irregular gill movement, or unusual swimming patterns due to parasites, it's crucial to seek veterinary help.

4. When to Seek Veterinary Help: If you notice the following symptoms, it is advisable to seek professional veterinary care:

- Persistent difficulty breathing or mouth breathing
- Severe gill swelling or discoloration
- Abnormal behavior such as continuous hiding or lethargy

- If natural remedies and water adjustments don't lead to improvement

A veterinarian with experience in fish health will be able to provide a thorough diagnosis and recommend the appropriate treatment to restore your piranha's health.

Respiratory and gill health are critical for the well-being of your piranha. By maintaining optimal water quality, monitoring for signs of distress, and using both natural and medical treatments when necessary, you can ensure that your piranha thrives in a healthy environment. Early detection and proactive care are key to preventing respiratory issues from becoming serious problems, allowing your piranha to live a long and healthy life.

Chapter 10: Dealing with Behavioral Issues and Stress

Identifying Causes of Stress and Aggression in Piranhas

Piranhas are naturally territorial and sometimes aggressive, especially in the wild, where they compete for resources and defend their territories. In the controlled environment of a home aquarium, several factors can cause stress or trigger aggression in your piranhas. Understanding these triggers and addressing them early can help maintain a peaceful and healthy environment for your pet.

1. **Common Causes of Stress:**

- **Poor Water Quality:** When water quality deteriorates, piranhas can become stressed and more prone to aggression. Ammonia, nitrites, and nitrates in the water can irritate their skin and gills, leading to a rise in stress levels.
- **Overcrowding:** Piranhas need sufficient space to establish their territory. A tank that is too small or overcrowded can cause territorial disputes, increased stress, and even aggressive behavior.
- **Incompatible Tank Mates:** Piranhas are carnivorous and can be territorial, so introducing smaller fish or incompatible species may result in aggression. Tank mates that invade their space can provoke stress and territorial aggression.
- **Lack of Hiding Spots:** In the wild, piranhas can hide among plants or underwater structures. In an aquarium, the absence of hiding spots can make them feel vulnerable and increase stress levels.
- **Temperature Fluctuations:** Sudden or extreme changes in water temperature can be stressful for piranhas, disrupting their normal behavior and increasing aggression.
- **Inadequate Diet or Hunger:** Hunger can trigger aggressive behavior, especially in competitive feeding scenarios. A lack of essential nutrients or a poor diet can cause discomfort and stress, potentially leading to aggressive interactions.

2. **Identifying Aggression:** Aggression in piranhas can manifest in several ways:

- **Biting and Nipping:** Piranhas may bite or nip at each other, especially during feeding time or when they feel threatened. This is a common behavior, but excessive biting or fighting can indicate stress or territory disputes.
- **Chasing:** Aggressive chasing behaviors can occur when piranhas are defending their territory or competing for food. This behavior can lead to physical injuries if not addressed.
- **Fighting and Fin Damage:** If aggression escalates, it can result in fighting, leading to injuries like torn fins or missing scales. Injuries caused by aggression can make a piranha more vulnerable to infection and further stress.
- **Isolation:** Some piranhas may become overly stressed and isolate themselves from the group, exhibiting abnormal swimming behavior or staying hidden for extended periods.

Creating a Stress-Free Environment

A calm and well-maintained environment is essential to prevent stress and aggression in your piranhas. By addressing potential stress factors and providing an enriched tank environment, you can reduce the likelihood of behavioral issues.

1. **Optimizing Tank Size and Layout:**

    - **Tank Size:** Ensure that your piranha's tank is large enough to allow for territory establishment and freedom of movement. A 75-gallon tank is recommended for a single piranha, with additional space for each new fish. Larger tanks help prevent overcrowding and offer more hiding spots and territories.
    - **Hiding Spots:** Adding plants, caves, rocks, and other decorations will provide piranhas with places to retreat when they feel threatened. This will give them the option to create personal space, reducing stress and territorial aggression.
    - **Surface Area:** Ensure that the tank has adequate surface area for piranhas to swim freely, as cramped spaces can increase aggression. Piranhas are active swimmers and require space to express their natural behaviors.

2. **Maintaining Water Quality:** Regular water maintenance is essential to keep stress levels low:

    - **Filtration:** Use a high-quality filtration system to maintain clean water. Piranhas are sensitive to poor water quality, and excess waste or toxins can lead to stress and health problems.
    - **Temperature Control:** Keep the water temperature stable and within the recommended range (75-80°F or 24-27°C). Sudden changes in temperature can shock your piranha and lead to stress.
    - **Water Changes:** Perform regular water changes (20-30% weekly) to keep water quality at optimal levels. Consistent water changes help prevent the accumulation of ammonia, nitrites, and nitrates, which can stress your piranha.

3. **Managing Tank Mates:** When adding tank mates, be selective to ensure compatibility with your piranha's temperament:

    - **Appropriate Tank Mates:** Larger, more robust species that do not compete for food or invade the piranha's space are ideal. Some potential tank mates include larger catfish, plecos, or other species that are not aggressive or territorial.
    - **Avoiding Smaller Fish:** Small fish may be viewed as prey by your piranha, and attempting to house them together can result in aggressive chasing or attacks.
    - **Socializing Piranhas:** Piranhas are territorial by nature, and introducing them to other piranhas can sometimes trigger aggressive behavior. It's best to introduce them slowly and in a controlled environment, allowing the fish to adjust to each other's presence.

Behavior Management Strategies and Holistic Calming Remedies

There are several behavior management strategies and holistic remedies that can help manage aggression and reduce stress in your piranhas. These approaches focus on addressing the root causes of stress and promoting relaxation without relying solely on medical interventions.

1. **Reducing Stress Through Environmental Enrichment:**

    - **Adding Visual Barriers:** Installing visual barriers in the tank can help reduce territorial disputes between piranhas. Adding plants or aquarium structures that block the view of other fish can prevent constant visual contact and reduce stress.
    - **Providing Hiding Spots:** Adding caves or shelters allows piranhas to retreat to safe spaces when they feel overwhelmed or threatened. This reduces the chance of aggressive behavior triggered by territoriality.

- **Maintaining a Consistent Routine:** Piranhas, like most fish, benefit from a predictable environment. Feed them at the same time each day, keep water changes on a regular schedule, and maintain a consistent lighting schedule. Predictability can help reduce anxiety and stress in piranhas.

2. Natural Calming Remedies:

- **Herbal Additives:** Certain herbal additives, like **valerian root** or **chamomile**, have natural calming effects. These can be added to the water in small amounts or used in tank treatments to help calm the piranhas. However, always ensure that the additives are safe for aquarium use and do not harm the fish.
- **Aromatherapy:** Although unconventional in fishkeeping, some fish owners use essential oils (like **lavender**) placed outside the tank in a diffuser to promote calm in the fish. The gentle aroma may have a mild sedative effect that reduces stress.
- **Meditation and Calm Music:** Some piranha owners have reported that playing gentle, soothing music or white noise near the tank can reduce stress and aggression. This may help create a more relaxed environment for the fish.

3. **Nutrition and Stress Reduction:** Proper nutrition plays a significant role in your piranha's emotional well-being. A balanced diet will not only prevent hunger-induced aggression but also provide the necessary nutrients to keep the fish healthy and resilient to stress.

- **High-Quality Diet:** Feed your piranhas a diet rich in protein, including fresh or frozen meat (e.g., fish, shrimp, or earthworms). Offer a variety of foods to keep them satisfied and reduce the likelihood of aggression during feeding time.
- **Supplements:** Consider adding natural supplements like **spirulina** or **garlic** to their diet to boost their immune system and reduce stress. These supplements also promote overall health and can help manage minor behavioral issues.

When Behavior May Require Veterinary Care

Although most behavioral issues can be managed with environmental adjustments and holistic remedies, some situations may require professional intervention. In these cases, a veterinarian specializing in fish health can provide a thorough diagnosis and recommend treatments.

1. Signs that Require Professional Help:

- **Severe Aggression:** If your piranha exhibits continuous or severe aggression toward other tank mates (including biting, tearing fins, or killing other fish), it may require a veterinary consultation. The vet may check for underlying health issues, such as hormonal imbalances or neurological problems.
- **Chronic Stress:** If your piranha seems to be constantly stressed despite environmental changes, it may be suffering from an underlying health condition, such as parasites or infections, that exacerbates stress.
- **Behavioral Changes Due to Illness:** Sometimes, aggression or unusual behavior can be a sign of a medical issue, such as pain from an injury or infection. If you notice a sudden, drastic change in behavior, such as unresponsiveness or aggression that doesn't subside, it's essential to seek veterinary advice.
- **Unexplained Weight Loss or Appetite Loss:** Stress can lead to appetite loss, but if your piranha is showing prolonged signs of weight loss or has stopped eating altogether, it could be a sign of a deeper health issue that

requires veterinary attention.

Managing stress and aggression in piranhas is essential for maintaining a healthy and harmonious aquarium environment. By understanding the causes of stress and aggression, providing a suitable tank setup, and incorporating holistic remedies, you can promote a calm and stress-free atmosphere for your piranhas. If behavioral issues persist or escalate, don't hesitate to consult with a veterinarian to ensure your piranhas receive the care they need for their emotional and physical well-being.

Chapter 11: Reproductive Health and Care for Breeding Piranhas

The Basics of Breeding Piranhas

Breeding piranhas in captivity can be a rewarding but challenging experience. In the wild, piranhas typically breed during the rainy season, when they have access to abundant food and suitable water conditions. In an aquarium setting, creating the right conditions for breeding requires careful attention to their environment, diet, and health.

1. Understanding Piranha Reproduction: Piranhas are generally considered to be monogamous during breeding season. They form pairs, with a male and a female working together to build a nest. During mating, the female lays eggs, which the male fertilizes. The eggs hatch into fry, which both parents protect until they are strong enough to fend for themselves.

Piranhas can start breeding at around 2-3 years old, though this can vary based on species and environmental conditions. Before attempting to breed your piranhas, it's important to understand the behaviors and physical signs of readiness to breed.

2. Signs of Breeding Readiness:

- **Increased Aggression:** During the breeding season, the male piranha becomes more territorial and aggressive, often chasing the female around the tank.
- **Physical Changes:** Females may appear rounder or larger when they are ready to lay eggs. Male piranhas may develop more vibrant coloring or specific physical traits, such as a slightly larger head or more defined fins, during breeding season.
- **Nesting Behavior:** Male piranhas often begin digging pits in the substrate or creating small clearing areas where the female will lay her eggs. These nests are usually built near tank decorations or plants.

Environmental Setup for Successful Breeding

Creating the ideal environment for breeding piranhas is crucial to success. Piranhas, like many fish species, require specific conditions for successful mating and the health of their fry.

1. Tank Size and Layout: A breeding tank should be at least 75 gallons for a pair of piranhas. However, if you plan on housing multiple pairs, you will need a much larger setup to accommodate their territorial nature. A well-sized tank allows the pair to establish their own space, reducing stress and aggression.

- **Substrate:** Use a fine-gravel or sandy substrate, which makes it easier for the piranhas to create nests. Avoid using sharp rocks that can injure the fish or disrupt their nest-building process.
- **Plants and Decorations:** While piranhas are carnivorous, providing plants or artificial caves can help create a more natural and comfortable environment. These spaces can serve as hiding spots for the female while she prepares to lay her eggs. The male will often guard these areas fiercely.
- **Water Quality and Filtration:** Maintaining high water quality is critical during the breeding process. The water should be clean and free from toxins, with a consistent filtration system. Ensure that there is minimal movement in the water, as piranhas prefer calm, stable environments when breeding.
- **Water Temperature and pH:** To encourage breeding, adjust the water temperature to between 80-82°F

(27-28°C). Piranhas prefer slightly acidic water with a pH of 6.5 to 7.5. Sudden fluctuations in temperature or pH levels can lead to stress and failure to breed.

2. Lighting: Piranhas respond to the natural light cycle, so ensure that the tank is exposed to 10-12 hours of light per day. You can use aquarium lights with a timer to simulate a natural day-night cycle. Too much light can stress the fish, while insufficient lighting can disrupt their natural behavior and breeding readiness.

3. Feeding Prior to Breeding: To encourage breeding, ensure that your piranhas receive a high-protein diet prior to and during the breeding season. Offer a variety of fresh or frozen foods, such as fish, shrimp, and earthworms, which are rich in nutrients. Feeding them well in advance can help stimulate their reproductive instincts.

Caring for Fry and Managing Post-Breeding Health

Once your piranhas have successfully bred, the real challenge begins. Caring for the fry and managing the health of the parents during and after the breeding process requires careful monitoring and support.

1. Post-Breeding Behavior: After fertilization, the female will lay her eggs on a clean substrate, often near the nest the male created. The male piranha will guard the eggs fiercely, while the female may help in protecting the nest. It is not uncommon for one parent to guard the eggs while the other hunts for food. This behavior continues until the fry hatch.

- **Hatching:** Piranha eggs typically hatch within 3-4 days, depending on water temperature and conditions. The fry will be small and fragile, requiring a safe environment free from threats.
- **Fry Care:** Once hatched, the fry will rely on their yolk sacs for nourishment for the first few days. Once they begin to swim and search for food, you can start offering finely chopped food, such as brine shrimp or specially formulated fry food.

2. Parental Care of Fry: During the early stages of development, the parents will guard the fry. The male may chase away other fish or threats, while the female often stays close to the fry. However, piranha parents can become aggressive, especially when protecting their young. It's important to give them space during this time to avoid disturbing them.

3. Separating Fry for Safety: As the fry grow, they will become increasingly independent, but may still be at risk of being eaten by the adult piranhas or other tank mates. If you notice aggressive behavior towards the fry, it may be necessary to move the fry into a separate nursery tank. This can be a smaller tank with the same water conditions, ensuring the fry are kept safe while they continue to grow.

4. Post-Breeding Health Monitoring: Breeding can take a toll on both the male and female piranha. It's essential to monitor their health closely after breeding. Look for signs of stress, injury, or disease, particularly in the female, who may become exhausted or weakened after the intense energy expenditure involved in spawning.

- **Signs of Stress or Illness:** Common symptoms to watch for in the post-breeding period include loss of appetite, lethargy, discolored or ragged fins, and unusual swimming behavior. If these signs persist, consider consulting a veterinarian to ensure the health of the fish.
- **Nutrition After Breeding:** Continue to feed the piranhas high-protein, nutritious food to help them recover from the breeding process. Proper post-breeding care can help prevent nutritional deficiencies or stress-related illnesses.

Holistic and Medical Treatments for Reproductive Health

Supporting the reproductive health of your piranhas involves both holistic and medical approaches. Maintaining the right environment, diet, and overall health can ensure that your fish remain in good condition during the breeding process.

1. **Holistic Approaches to Reproductive Health:**

- **Herbal Additives:** Certain herbs like **garlic** can help boost the immune system of breeding fish. Adding a small amount of garlic to the tank can help improve the overall health of your piranhas and reduce the likelihood of infection.
- **Epsom Salt Baths:** In some cases, an Epsom salt bath can help relieve stress and improve overall health, particularly after breeding. Epsom salt can help with muscle relaxation and reduce the risk of infection from stress-related injuries.

2. **Medical Treatments:** If your piranhas are showing signs of illness during the breeding process, such as abnormal swimming, lethargy, or external injuries, medical intervention may be required. Common treatments include:

- **Antibiotics:** If your piranha develops a bacterial infection after breeding (for example, a skin injury or fin rot), a veterinarian may recommend topical or oral antibiotics to prevent the infection from spreading.
- **Anti-parasitic Treatments:** Sometimes, parasites like **ich** or **external worms** can affect breeding piranhas. A vet can prescribe treatments for parasites, ensuring that both the parents and fry remain healthy.
- **Hormonal Injections:** In rare cases, breeders may use hormonal injections to induce breeding in piranhas. These are typically administered under the guidance of an experienced veterinarian and are only used in certain situations where natural breeding attempts have failed.

Breeding piranhas can be a complex process, but with the right setup, care, and attention to their reproductive health, it can be incredibly rewarding. Understanding the basics of piranha reproduction, creating an ideal environment for breeding, and offering proper care for both the fry and the parents are crucial steps in ensuring success. Whether you choose a holistic or medical approach to managing reproductive health, the key is to maintain a balance that supports the health and well-being of your piranhas throughout the breeding cycle.

Chapter 12: Bonus Recipes for Piranha Health

Natural Feeding Options and Treats

Piranhas are carnivorous by nature, and their diet should focus on high-protein, animal-based foods. However, by adding natural, whole foods to their diet, you can provide additional nutrients that promote overall health. Below are some recipes for natural feeding options and treats:

1. Fish-Based Protein Treats: Fish is a natural and essential food for piranhas. You can prepare various types of fish-based treats that your piranha will love.

- **Recipe: Fish & Shrimp Medley**
    - Ingredients: Fresh fish fillets (such as tilapia or cod), fresh shrimp (shelled and deveined).
    - Preparation: Chop the fish fillets and shrimp into small, bite-sized pieces. Place them in a blender with a small amount of water and blend until a paste is formed.
    - Serving: Freeze the mixture in ice cube trays for easy portion control. Defrost and serve as a protein-packed treat.
- **Recipe: Fish and Squid Mix**
    - Ingredients: Fresh squid, fish fillets, fish oil.
    - Preparation: Dice the squid and fish into small chunks. Blend them together with a tablespoon of fish oil.
    - Serving: Freeze in molds and offer small portions to your piranha every 3-4 days.

2. Gelatin Fish Food: Gelatin is a great way to bind natural ingredients into a simple and nutritious treat that holds its form underwater.

- **Recipe: Gelatin Fish Patties**
    - Ingredients: 2 tbsp gelatin, 1 cup fish stock, 1/2 cup chopped shrimp, 1/2 cup spinach (finely chopped), 1/4 cup fish meal or powdered fish.
    - Preparation: Dissolve the gelatin in the fish stock. Mix in the shrimp, spinach, and fish meal. Pour the mixture into silicone molds or a shallow pan and refrigerate until set.
    - Serving: Once set, break into small portions and feed 2-3 times per week.

3. Protein-Rich Insects: Insects are an excellent source of protein and mimic the natural diet of piranhas in the wild.

- **Recipe: Insect Protein Balls**
    - Ingredients: Crickets or mealworms (dried or live), mashed salmon, fish oil.
    - Preparation: Grind the crickets or mealworms into a fine powder. Mix with mashed salmon and a bit of fish oil until you form a sticky dough.
    - Serving: Roll into small balls and freeze for later use. Serve as an occasional treat for added protein.

Homemade Supplements for a Healthy Diet

Incorporating homemade supplements into your piranha's diet can help boost their immune system, support digestion, and enhance overall health. Below are some simple supplements you can make at home using natural ingredients.

1. Immune-Boosting Supplement: A strong immune system is essential for preventing diseases and infections. This supplement helps boost your piranha's immunity.

- **Recipe: Garlic and Fish Oil Supplement**
    - Ingredients: Fresh garlic, fish oil.
    - Preparation: Crush a small clove of garlic and mix it with 1 tablespoon of fish oil. Let it sit for a few hours to allow the garlic to infuse.
    - Serving: Add 1-2 drops of the mixture to your piranha's regular food every 1-2 weeks to support their immune system.

2. Digestive Health Supplement: A healthy digestive system is crucial for nutrient absorption and overall well-being.

- **Recipe: Pumpkin and Papaya Mix**
    - Ingredients: Fresh pumpkin, fresh papaya, a pinch of spirulina.
    - Preparation: Puree equal amounts of pumpkin and papaya. Mix in a pinch of spirulina powder for added nutrients.
    - Serving: Add this supplement to your piranha's food once or twice a week to aid digestion.

3. Stress-Relief Supplement: Stress can lead to health problems such as poor eating habits and aggression. This supplement helps promote relaxation.

- **Recipe: Chamomile and Lavender Infusion**
    - Ingredients: Dried chamomile flowers, dried lavender, distilled water.
    - Preparation: Boil 1 cup of distilled water and steep 1 teaspoon each of chamomile and lavender. Let it cool and strain.
    - Serving: Add a few drops of the infused water to your piranha's food once a week to reduce stress and promote calm.

Recipe Tips for Improving Digestion, Immune Health, and Stress Relief

1. Digestion-Friendly Foods: Piranhas, like all animals, benefit from foods that help regulate their digestive system. High-fiber ingredients like pumpkin and papaya can be very helpful. Incorporate these ingredients into your piranha's diet regularly to promote better digestion.

- Use fiber-rich foods like pumpkin puree, spirulina, or even small amounts of well-cooked carrots in homemade food preparations.
- Make sure that any food prepared is finely chopped or ground, as piranhas may have difficulty digesting large chunks of food.

2. Immune System Boosters: Your piranha's immune system can be enhanced with a diet that includes antioxidant-rich foods. Garlic, papaya, and spirulina are all great choices.

- Add small amounts of garlic and vitamin-rich vegetables to their food to support immune health.
- Incorporate fish oil into their diet for healthy fats and omega-3 fatty acids, which can also aid in immune function.

3. Stress Reduction: Piranhas can experience stress from changes in the tank environment, water conditions, or even interaction with other fish. A calming supplement can help relieve this.

- Offer chamomile or lavender-based treats that promote relaxation. These herbs have mild sedative properties that can be useful during stressful periods, such as tank changes or water quality fluctuations.
- Make sure the tank environment is peaceful and free of stressors, as even the healthiest diet cannot fix stress caused by environmental instability.

Additional Tips for Holistic Feeding

- **Variety is Key:** Even though piranhas are carnivorous, it's important to offer a variety of food options to ensure they get a wide range of nutrients. Experiment with different protein sources such as fish, shrimp, or insects to keep their diet interesting and diverse.
- **Monitor for Overfeeding:** Piranhas are notorious for their aggressive feeding habits, but overfeeding can lead to obesity, poor water quality, and health problems. Always provide food in appropriate portions, and remove any uneaten food promptly to avoid tank contamination.
- **Consistency and Timing:** Consistency in feeding is important. Regular feeding schedules will help keep your piranha's metabolism stable and prevent overeating or underfeeding. Offer food 2-3 times a week with occasional treats or supplements.

With these 100+ recipes and tips for holistic care, you can confidently provide your piranha with a nutritious and balanced diet that promotes long-term health and well-being. These recipes allow you to support your fish's needs with simple, natural ingredients that benefit their digestion, immunity, and overall happiness. By incorporating both natural feeding options and homemade supplements, you can ensure that your piranha thrives in a healthy and supportive environment.

Chapter 13: 30-Day Piranha Care Plan

Caring for a piranha requires a thoughtful, consistent approach to ensure its health and well-being. The following 30-day care plan breaks down the daily, weekly, and monthly tasks needed to keep your piranha healthy, happy, and thriving. Regular health monitoring, preventive care, and attention to behavioral changes will help you spot potential issues early and maintain a stable, healthy environment.

Daily Care Tasks

Daily care tasks are essential for maintaining a healthy tank environment, ensuring your piranha's health, and preventing minor issues from escalating.

1. Feed Your Piranha Properly:

- Provide fresh, appropriate food based on your piranha's nutritional needs (e.g., fish fillets, shrimp, or natural treats). Be sure to feed in moderation to prevent overfeeding and maintain water quality.
- Remove any uneaten food promptly to avoid water contamination and to maintain tank cleanliness.

2. Water Quality Check:

- **Check the temperature:** Ensure the water temperature is stable between 75°F and 82°F (24°C - 28°C). Fluctuations can stress your piranha and lead to health problems.
- **Check the pH:** Piranhas prefer slightly acidic to neutral pH levels (6.5-7.5). Regularly check the pH and adjust if necessary.
- **Monitor ammonia, nitrites, and nitrates:** Ensure that ammonia and nitrite levels are at 0, and nitrate levels stay below 20 ppm. Perform water tests every day if you're monitoring tank conditions closely.

3. Visual Health Check:

- Observe your piranha for signs of distress or abnormal behavior, such as erratic swimming, discoloration, or lesions. These could be indicators of a potential health issue.
- Check for injuries or signs of aggression (especially if you keep more than one piranha in the tank).

4. Monitor Behavior:

- Take note of any behavioral changes, such as aggression, lethargy, or stress-related behaviors. Early detection of unusual behavior can help prevent bigger issues.
- Interact gently with your piranha if it is comfortable, as this helps reduce stress and create a bond.

Weekly Care Tasks

Weekly care tasks focus on maintaining the cleanliness of the tank, tracking any changes in the piranha's behavior, and supporting its long-term health.

1. Clean the Aquarium:

- **Water Change:** Perform a 20-30% water change weekly to maintain water quality. This helps to reduce toxins like ammonia, nitrites, and nitrates that accumulate in the tank.
- **Clean Filter:** Clean the filter as per the manufacturer's guidelines, ensuring that it is functioning optimally and does not have any clogs.
- **Scrub Surfaces:** Gently scrub the sides of the aquarium, decorations, and substrate to remove algae and any buildup of organic material.

2. **Check Tank Setup:**

- Assess the tank setup to ensure that the decor, plants, and substrate are in good condition. Make sure there are no sharp edges that could harm your piranha.
- Ensure that there are hiding spots available for your piranha, especially if it shares the tank with other fish. Piranhas can be territorial, and having a retreat space can reduce stress.

3. **Monitor Food Intake:**

- Keep a log of what and how much your piranha is eating. This will help you track if it's consistently eating the right portions and adjusting to its diet.

4. **Health Check:**

- Conduct a weekly visual health check (look for fin rot, skin issues, or parasites) and check for changes in weight or size. This helps detect problems early.

5. **Record Behavior:**

- Track your piranha's behavior changes, including aggression, lethargy, or unusual swimming patterns. Keep a record of any behavioral trends for better understanding.

Monthly Care Tasks

Monthly tasks are less frequent but crucial for maintaining your piranha's health and ensuring long-term sustainability.

1. **Full Water Quality Check:**

- Test all water parameters (ammonia, nitrites, nitrates, pH, hardness, and temperature) to ensure your piranha's tank conditions are stable and suitable for its health.
- Clean the substrate thoroughly, if necessary, but avoid removing too much beneficial bacteria.

2. **Update Care Plan:**

- Evaluate your piranha's overall health and behavior over the past month. If you've noticed any health or behavioral issues, now is the time to adjust the care plan or consult a veterinarian.
- Make any changes to the tank setup, feeding plan, or health routine based on observations from the past month.

3. Review Health Monitoring Records:

- Look through your health and behavior logs for any patterns or concerns that may need to be addressed. This is important for identifying recurring issues and making adjustments.

4. Check for Injuries or Signs of Disease:

- Examine the piranha carefully for any new or lingering injuries, infections, or signs of disease. Seek veterinary care if necessary.

Health Monitoring and Record-Keeping

Creating a health and care record for your piranha is an essential part of monitoring its health. This allows you to track its progress and identify any patterns that may suggest illness or discomfort.

1. Keep a Daily Log:

- Record any changes in behavior, feeding patterns, or health. Include details such as feeding times, portion sizes, and any water quality fluctuations.
- Note any signs of stress or aggression in the tank. Tracking these will help you identify trends.

2. Weekly Updates:

- Review your water quality tests and behavior notes each week. Make sure you're keeping an accurate record of your piranha's health and environment.

3. Monthly Reviews:

- At the end of each month, review your logs to ensure that your piranha is progressing well. If there are signs of ill health, this is the time to consult a veterinarian.

Preventive Care and Emergency Preparedness

1. Preventive Care:

- Preventive care is crucial to keep your piranha healthy. This includes proper water maintenance, regular feeding, and monitoring for stress or aggression.
- Use natural remedies or supplements to promote health but always ensure the water quality and diet are balanced.
- Keep your piranha's environment as stress-free as possible by maintaining stable water parameters and offering hiding spots.

2. Emergency Preparedness:

- In case of an emergency, such as a disease outbreak or sudden injury, be prepared with the following:
    - A quarantine tank to isolate a sick piranha.
    - Emergency treatments such as antibiotics or antifungal treatments, and know when to seek veterinary assistance.
    - Emergency contact information for a trusted aquatic veterinarian in your area.

Tracking Behavioral Changes and Development
1. Monitor Aggression:

- Aggression is a common issue with piranhas. Track changes in aggression levels and whether the piranha is becoming more territorial. If aggression increases, try adjusting the tank environment or consider keeping the piranha in a single-species setup.

2. Observe Social Dynamics:

- If your piranha is housed with other fish, observe how it interacts with them. Aggressive behavior can sometimes be managed by ensuring plenty of hiding spots and retreat areas.

3. Stress and Comfort Levels:

- Piranhas, like all fish, can experience stress from various factors, including tank conditions and interaction with other fish. Keep a close eye on behavior like rapid swimming, fin clamping, or refusal to eat. These signs indicate stress that needs to be addressed.

With this comprehensive 30-day care plan, you will be prepared to ensure the health and well-being of your piranha. By regularly performing daily, weekly, and monthly tasks, keeping detailed records, and remaining vigilant about potential health and behavioral issues, your piranha will thrive in a well-maintained, stress-free environment.

Chapter 14: FAQs and Additional Resources for Piranha Owners

Frequently Asked Questions on Piranha Care

1. How often should I feed my piranha?

- **Answer:** Piranhas should be fed once or twice a day, depending on their size and age. Adults typically eat once a day, while younger piranhas may require more frequent feedings. Always remove uneaten food to avoid water contamination.

2. What type of food should I feed my piranha?

- **Answer:** Piranhas are carnivorous, and their diet should consist primarily of animal-based proteins such as fish fillets, shrimp, worms, or specially formulated piranha pellets. Occasionally, you can provide natural treats like insects or other fresh meats. It's important to vary their diet to ensure they receive all necessary nutrients.

3. Can piranhas live with other fish?

- **Answer:** Piranhas can sometimes be kept with other fish, but caution is needed due to their territorial nature and aggressive tendencies. It's best to house them with similarly-sized, non-aggressive species. Avoid smaller fish, as they may become prey. Monitoring the tank's social dynamics is essential.

4. How big should the aquarium be for my piranha?

- **Answer:** The minimum recommended tank size for a single piranha is 30 gallons. For multiple piranhas or larger species, consider a tank size of 50 gallons or more. The larger the tank, the better for maintaining water quality and reducing aggression between tank mates.

5. Why is my piranha showing signs of aggression?

- **Answer:** Piranhas are naturally territorial, and aggression can result from factors such as overcrowding, insufficient hiding spots, or incompatible tank mates. Reducing stress, providing plenty of space, and ensuring a stable tank environment can help manage aggression.

6. How do I tell if my piranha is sick?

- **Answer:** Common signs of illness include abnormal swimming patterns, lack of appetite, discoloration, fin damage, or unusual behavior. If you notice any of these symptoms, perform a water quality test, check for external injuries, and consult a veterinarian if necessary.

7. What water parameters are best for my piranha?

- **Answer:** Piranhas thrive in slightly acidic to neutral water with a pH of 6.5-7.5. The ideal temperature range is between 75°F and 82°F (24°C - 28°C). Regularly monitor the levels of ammonia, nitrites, and nitrates to maintain a healthy aquatic environment.

8. How do I handle piranha aggression during feeding time?

- **Answer:** To reduce aggression during feeding, consider feeding your piranha in a separate feeding container or using a feeding stick. This method helps to avoid territorial disputes and allows each fish to have its portion of food without interference.

9. Are piranhas suitable pets for beginners?

- **Answer:** While piranhas can make fascinating pets, they are not the best choice for beginners due to their specific care requirements, aggressive nature, and need for a large, properly-maintained tank. New pet owners should ensure they are fully prepared to meet the needs of a piranha before committing to care.

Troubleshooting Common Issues
1. Water Quality Issues (Ammonia, Nitrites, Nitrates)

- **Problem:** High levels of ammonia, nitrites, or nitrates can harm your piranha and lead to stress, illness, or even death.
- **Solution:** Regularly test your water and perform partial water changes if necessary. Ensure that your filtration system is adequate and functioning properly. A consistent cleaning schedule is essential to keep toxin levels under control.

2. Aggression Between Tank Mates

- **Problem:** Piranhas are territorial by nature and may attack tank mates, especially if the tank is overcrowded or lacks hiding spots.
- **Solution:** Consider separating overly aggressive piranhas into their own tanks or adjusting the tank layout to provide more space and retreats. Keep fewer piranhas together to reduce territorial disputes.

3. Piranha Not Eating

- **Problem:** If your piranha refuses to eat, it may be stressed, unwell, or adjusting to a new environment.
- **Solution:** Check the water parameters for any imbalances, provide varied foods, and ensure the tank environment is suitable. If the piranha continues to refuse food, consult a veterinarian for a health check.

4. Skin or Fin Damage

- **Problem:** Piranhas can injure themselves during fights with other fish or against tank decorations.
- **Solution:** Provide ample hiding spots to reduce aggression. If an injury occurs, treat the wound with appropriate antifungal or antibacterial treatments. Keep the injured piranha in a quarantine tank if necessary.

5. Unhealthy Water Conditions

- **Problem:** Cloudy water or the presence of algae can indicate poor water quality, often due to overfeeding or a malfunctioning filter.
- **Solution:** Perform regular water changes, clean the substrate and filter, and avoid overfeeding. You may need to invest in a more powerful filtration system if your tank's water quality is constantly compromised.

6. Stress from Poor Tank Conditions

- **Problem:** Stress can manifest in erratic swimming, refusal to eat, or color fading. This may result from improper water temperature, poor water quality, or tank overcrowding.
- **Solution:** Ensure the water temperature is within the ideal range, perform regular water changes, and make sure your piranha has enough space to swim freely. Reduce environmental stressors by keeping the tank quiet and stable.

Additional Resources for Piranha Owners

To help you further navigate piranha care, here are some valuable resources:

1. Books and Articles:

- **"Piranha Care and Behavior"** – A detailed guide covering everything from basic piranha care to advanced topics like breeding and disease management.
- **"The Fishkeeping Bible"** – A comprehensive resource for all types of aquarium fish, including piranhas.

2. Online Communities:

- **Fishkeeping Forums:** Websites such as Fishlore.com and ThePiranhaTank.com offer a wealth of advice, support, and community insights from experienced piranha owners.
- **Social Media Groups:** There are many Facebook groups and Instagram accounts dedicated to piranha care, where owners share their experiences, tips, and photos.

3. Aquatic Veterinarians:

- When in doubt, consult with an experienced aquatic veterinarian. Many veterinary practices specialize in exotic fish care and can assist with diagnosing and treating common piranha ailments.

4. Local Fish Stores:

- Visit a reputable local fish store for advice on piranha care, purchasing equipment, and sourcing healthy food options.

This FAQ and troubleshooting section, along with the additional resources, should serve as a valuable tool to help you provide the best care possible for your piranha. With the right knowledge and support, you can ensure a long, healthy, and enjoyable life for your pet piranha.

Printed in Dunstable, United Kingdom